The Connection

by

Helene Montessigny-Clement

Order this book online at www.trafford.com
or email orders@trafford.com

Most Trafford titles are also available at major online book retailers.

Note for Librarians: A cataloguing record for this book is available from Library and Archives Canada at www.collectionscanada.ca/amicus/index-e.html

Printed in Victoria, BC, Canada.

ISBN: 978-1-4269-1724-0

Library of Congress Control Number: 2009935539

Our mission is to efficiently provide the world's finest, most comprehensive book publishing service, enabling every author to experience success. To find out how to publish your book, your way, and have it available worldwide, visit us online at www.trafford.com

Trafford rev. 09/08/09

www.trafford.com

North America & international
toll-free: 1 888 232 4444 (USA & Canada)
phone: 250 383 6864 ♦ fax: 812 355 4082

I dedicate this book to my Father.

Table of Contents

A Day in My Life

As if I was afraid to miss out
My morning starts early.
The beauty of rising sun on the prairie,
The scent of dew sparkling amidst grass.

The overwhelming open sky
Clear and blue like a child's eyes.
Someone placed me here to live,
I am in the very centre of it.

I am walking on warm earth,
My bare feet step on flowers,
They are bending and bowing to me,
Their welcoming fragrance so sweet.

Transfixed with the beauty of this land
I am floating in the air aghast.
The mewling, chirruping birds add up
To a grand image of Creator's art.

Wherever I go this beauty follows,
For I am an inseparable part of this world.
When everything else fails His image will last,
Will nurture and be the final accord.

A Kiedy Zagraja Nam

Gdy smuce sie i dawne czasy wspominam,
Lzy do oczu naplywaja, siadam przy lampie zapalonej,
Slucham muzyki Szopena,
I na nowo wszystko przezywam.

Lata srogie wojny przeszly,
Niedostatkow i cierpien niezliczonych,
Opresji, ruin domow i przesladowan,
Walki o byt twardej i rzadow narzuconych.

Smutna nuta drga i w mojej duszy krwawi,
Dzwieczy i dzwiga moje rozterki.
Zasluchana w berceuse Szopena nic nie pamietam,
Cala w sobie sie pale.

Gdy w powstaniu sierpniowym surmy bojowe zagraly
Najmlodsi z mlodych do boju sie porwali.
Nierowna to, ciezko okupiona walka byla,
A oni z piersia otwarta szli. I w szeregu padali.

Ich serca mlode, pelne milosci do ojczyzny
I prezne ramiona stawione na barykadach,
Na zawsze pozostana w kamiennych tablicach,
Zyc beda w klosach zboz, na polnych miedzach.

Polsko, badz dumna z mlodych.
Oni swe zycie na szancu polozyli.
Abysmy mogli ten kraj kochac i chwalic
I w mazurkach Szopena go budowali.

Again

I am walking, my feet heavy,
Not seeing much, head in the clouds.
A burden of life on my shoulders,
I am bent and weary.

I meet my love unexpectedly,
Everything has been lifted, changed.
Again, I can see beautiful birds around,
I can smell lilac and jasmine to full extent.

Again and again, I'm alive.
I've got an unlimited power to love,
Given to me from the sky, a special grace,
For I have to go on, it makes a perfect sense.

My world is full of promise,
My heart stopped aching, it feels so light,
Cause I am empowered with true love
That gives me wings to fly.

I have to go on and love
Turning my back on the past.
Nothing is more important than this,
The very essence of life.

Berceuse

The notes, quiet, relentless, appeasing,
Wandering across the sky.
Slowly, slowly, moving from star to star,
Reaching the bottom and again up.

The sounds, heavenly,
Getting straight through your heart.
Piercing it, cutting in half
Until it bleeds in agony and you're falling apart.

A caress, alluring, magnetic, angelic,
Whispering the promise, the unknown.
Ascending with light, then descending with a great charm
Until you fall to pieces, until you're spellbound.

Vibrating, resonating, they sound timeless,
Extraterrestrial, like diamonds dazzling, divine.
Crying, trembling, travelling in time,
Your thoughts and senses all aligned.

Freedom

Freedom, my Love, freedom...
Priceless, righteous, at birth given by God,
Above the gravity flying me,
Wings spread widely in victory.

Out of darkness it came like a miracle,
So suddenly; the greatest gift.
I stood in quiet astonishment, amazed, in disbelief,
I had it all along inside me.

I was given a true liberta,
All chains have been broken and abandoned,
The whole world shook and thundered
And carried that sound throughout.

My thoughts flow freely, unbound,
The wind lifts them up and all around.
There is no limit to my imagination,
I truly feel I am God's creation.

I will do seeding, watch the fields grow,
I will pass on words to the next generation,
For this country, my home, I will stand.
Oh Canada, my beloved free land.

Immortal

Like a leaf trembling, withering,
With cold air blast
That grips yesterday's beauty
And makes it a memory, I will be crushed.

To withstand an antagonism of fate
It takes someone's life,
To defend a beautiful innocence
Nothing can be more noble, just.

Not many allies around,
A struggle of memories past, hurting,
Pulling you down until it burns a hole inside.
True love, the only thing precious that counts.

It soothes all, makes you anew,
Means everything and fills your heart,
And when you tremble
It's in your soul and all around.

Build your dreams on it,
The golden threads, dazzling will be weaved in
The trembling leaves whispering a song,
Love, soft and strong. Immortal.

In Need

In your hands I place my fate
Mother of God, I humbly lay my plea,
I am at the crossroads,
Show me the direction, take care of me.

You gave me freedom, family,
In troubled times you always guided me.
When I stood by your feet
With gentle eyes you showed me your mercy.

When times got tough, when cornered,
Isolated and abandoned, grieving,
Helpless, searching -
You gave me strength, turned around my sorrows.

You've brought me to my apogee,
Showered me with all gifts.
I am a human because of your will,
Take my prayer for your Love and Divinity.

Jozef Pilsudski
Non Omnes Moriar

Tam, gdzie doliny i pagorki Niemen przecina,
Ciagnie sie i rozposciera kraj piekny
Ziemi zyznej, modlitwy porannej i przecudnych oblokow,
Miast i wsi zadbanych, na polskich motywach wychowanych.

Litwa, przez wieki z Polska unia polaczona
Wydala nam synow miary wielkiej,
Na ktorych Polska uciemiezona dlugo czekala,
A dzwony kosciolow wiadomosc nadejscia ich przepowiadaly.

W okrutnych czasach rosyjskich zaborow sie urodzil,
Syn z matki Polki, bohater narodu,
Z mrokow niewoli z szabla powstal,
A szlak jego czynow przez Warszawe na Krakow prowadzil.

Wodz nasz wielki, przez zaborcow latami wieziony,
Dla odrodzenia polskiej nacji ocalony,
Polskie Legiony na obczyznie stworzyl,
Aniol wolnosci przed nim szedl i jemu blogoslawil.

Na kon, na kon, do walki szli,
Wyrabac szabla wolnosc w bitwie do ostatniej kropli krwi,
By narod z niewoli wydzwignac,
By Polski narod zyl w niepodleglej Ojczyznie.

Jedyne haslo jak pochodnia im przyswiecalo,
Bog, honor i Ojczyzna.
Ogien wolnosci w nich sie zarzyl,
A lasy zielone i rzeki szumiace dla nich spiewaly.

Legiony polskie, duma narodu polskiego,
Za laska Pani Jasnogorskiej mocy
Przemierzaly polacie dniem i noca,
Mundury proste i czapki z orlem, symbolu naszego.

Ulani, ulani, malowane dzieci,
Wasza krew przelana za matki, ojcow,
Za nasz kraj w mekach udreczony,
Legenda o was trwa, nigdy nie zapomniana.

Wodzu wielki, Ty, ktory nasz kraj wlasna szabla wskrzesiles,
Jakiejz to potegi ducha i odwagi trzeba bylo...
Czesc serca swego
Wsrod polnych chabrow i makow na zawsze zostawiles...

Przez Opatrznosc dla nas wyznaczony,
Choc Bez Korony wsrod krolow jako krol pochowany,
Jak przyklad nam na wieki swiecisz,
A my nasz hold Ci oddajemy, narodu tego wierne dzieci.

Love in the Crowd

We dream we love,
When we are together.
We hold our breath
As the time ticks by.

We touch each other's hand
Walking on summer's fresh grass.
The leaves up above gently shake
Giving us a quiet praise.

Strangers walk by smiling,
Our happiness open, inviting,
They are drawn to us, connected,
An invisible sign of blessing.

We look forward to the future,
Angels are with us.
The time has stopped
So we can float.

Love in the Summer

Love, gentle and sweet like a rose petal,
You possessed me and my soul,
Holding me tightly
And I squirm trying to free myself.

I am a prisoner of my own feelings,
Getting deeper and deeper
Into an abyss, hardly breathing,
Falling into a bottomless state.

There are no thoughts,
Only sweet, soft spoken words,
Torn into pieces,
That interrupted, came out.

My senses shattered,
I know my love is returned.
The angels carry me,
My life fulfilled for eternity.

My Child

The eyes of my child,
Full of expression.
Looking at me with concern,
These beautiful, innocent blue eyes.

The hugs we give to each other,
Her words spoken with love,
Closeness of being for now
Will last till I last.

Her being was given to me,
My greatest gift in life.
The mother-daughter bond eternal,
The feelings overflown in our hearts.

Her love for me strong,
Helpful hands around.
The bond we share very special and untorn.
My deepest meaning of my life.

My Creed

When I dance I want the world to watch,
And when I sing I don't need accompaniment,
For this is my happy day,
I want to live it just this moment.

I wish the harmony of the moon and the sun,
Why wouldn't I if they are my guides.
And when I am lost, abandoned -
A friendly gesture will be enough.

I went through life loving and giving
To those close around me.
Some took and never gave back,
I was calling lonely, in a shock.

When I built my life with precision
To those that I cared about
I gave my greatest love and sole attention
So they could grow on aspiration.

And when I laugh and love
You get my genuine affection,
As I see the world in different dimensions,
For this is the essence of my being.

And when I am gone
I want you to remember only the good about me
That I put into your soul,
As to live, laugh and love was my creed.

Na Brata

Dziecinstwo - czasy beztroskie, kolorowe.
Zawsze widze rodzenstwo wokol,
Wspolne zabawy, ksiazki, lekcje i rozmowy,
A najwazniejsze - poczucie bepieczenstwa.

W kolysce lezac w ciezkiej chorobie,
Sasiedzi wraz z rodzina zamartwieni wokol
Bezradnosc dzielac, wspolny klopot,
Moj brat uchylil mi zycia jakby mlody sokol.

Maluchem bylam i za jego plecami wyroslam,
Zawsze z podziwem na niego patrzylam
Jakby na pedestal, Jak na wielki obraz.
Nawet kiedy klucz z gwozdziem wybuchl eksplozja.

A kiedy noge ciezko skaleczylam,
Brat moj swym bystrym okiem przeczul zagrozenie
I z matka do lekarza spieszyl
Aby ratowac mnie, takie bylo jego powolanie.

NAd siostra stoi dlugo, jej tlumaczy,
Do glowy wklada rozne iksy, delty i potegi.
TAki byl z niego super zdolny matematyk
I agronom, z glowa za pieciu, jak nie wiecej.

Rodzicow duma, a dla nas Zeus,
W szkole same laury i pochwaly zbieral,
I zapowiadal sie juz wtedy na ogromny talent,
A profesor Nemetti dlugo go pamietal.

Szkola morska wytyczyla jego droge,
A czar munduru podkreslal Zeusa urode.
“Wysoki jak dab”, dumny i z wizja,
Na przyszlosc patrzyl z podniesionym czolem.

A ja, zapatrzona w niego, wizje te przejelam,
Per aspera ad astra szlam i rzeczy dokonalam.
Moj cel - zdobywac, pomnazac, do gory isc, po mostach,
Z sukcesem wspinac sie w zycie. Droga prosta

Z usmiechem dzis do tych lat dzieciecych siegam.
RAdosne zabawy na podworku i dzieci sasiadow,
Wspolne rozmowy i kopanie kartofli, ciezkie.
Najlepsze wspolne lata - w mych slowach ich refleksje.

Wpojono mi zasady i swobode myslenia,
Nawet skrzetnego zlotowek liczenia.
I perspektywy na zas, do przodu, otwarcie.
Niejednokrotnie z budujaca krytyka i wsparciem.

Dar Pomorza to piekny polski okaz jachtu

Gdzie szkolono przyszlych nawigatorow na oficerskie wachty.
A na nas szkrabow brata splendor splywal..
" W podskokach " nabieralo sie zyciowgo rozmachu i perspektywy.

W retrospekcji tamtych lat refren sie odzywa,
Jak przyplyw i odplyw ciagle sie powtarza.
Dwa kontynenty i ocean pomiedzy nami,
Ale Canada dzwoni do Polski czesto, bez granic.

Papa, o Mio Caro - Beloved Father

The sound of trumpets,
A clear voice of tenor starts singing
Sweet, loud La Liberta'....
It has a special meaning, it's riveting my heart.

The words have stopped me and I shuddered,
I had them all this time in my soul embedded.
They have been resonating all along,
I have been struck with a tremendous force.

Papa lives in the song...
He can talk to His people as He always did.
Inconceivable, and yet His words are flowing...
What a great depth to them, so profoundly moving.

Papa, I remember when they elected Him
To be seated on the highest throne.
Tears ran steadily on my face
As on the faces of millions of Poles.

We held our breath deeply touched.
You were making a history in front of our eyes.
For the country in chains, bound,
Where freedom was not allowed.

Throughout the years of oppression we carried on,
When enemy powers scratched Poland off the map,
Through persecution, rejection and extermination we endured,
The times when Polish language and spirit only in prayers could survive.

The Divine face of Freedom and Love
Denied to people for century.
You had a vision and inspired us,
With you it awakened, it was coming.

You came as herald to us from Poland,
The uplifting words that we adore ever since
"Do Not Be Afraid" you had said
Transfixed our hearts, gave us strength, open a new age.

The seeds of wisdom had been sown...
The impossible became possible. You gave hope to the nation.
You'd crushed the fortresses of evil and oppression
And we have reaped what you had sowed.

Your radiant, angelic face and thoughtful eyes...
You had reached out to poor of all human race,
You gave the dignity back to working man,
Children had in your heart always a special place.

Freedom, You knew it all along,
Is priceless.
You took us by surprise
When you breathed in those words into our souls.

Son of Polish nation, Pilgrim,
You had abolished evil powers.
Your graceful hand and the white robe
Was a sign from the Almighty God.

You followed teachings of Cardinal Sapieha,
Cardinal Wyszynski was Your dear mentor.
In times of WWII, You, as all the people suffered,
Never giving up Hope and Faith but building character.

You spoke Your mind,
Deeply from Your thought and faith,
You stood bravely, to thousands were undefeated,
The people shuddered under Your prayer, courage and divinity.

"Goralu, czy Ci nie zal,
Goralu, wracaj do hal "
They chanted long into the night,
To show You an outpouring of faith, affection and love.

You were raised in our darkest hour,
When times were getting tough, when there was only sorrow,
The country suppressed, in turmoil,
When there was anything but hope and tomorrow.

We grieve, we feel a profound sorrow.
You've performed Your duties as Vicar of Christ.
It's hard to say good-bye...
Your wisdom and love we will always follow, always follow...

Saturday's Promise

All in one day, the momentum of us,
It's hard to measure its weight,
Make it compact and lock it
Last for a week and again wait.

The apple twigs in pink blossoms,
The scent of earth and green fields.
And us, in the centre
Of God's creation. Living the dream.

We take the road whatever it may be
And embrace all we are given,
Holding each other close,
Being for now, tomorrow, in unison.

Two souls, we've found each other,
To live the time, to last, to shine.
A dream came true and goes on
And we're entangled. In promise entwined.

Tears

Weary and tired, head down,
She's sitting among the crowd.
The passers-by go in their own direction,
Nobody pays to the girl's tears attention.

The shape of leaf in water
Seen through the glass,
Like woman's face in tears,
Transparent, just does not mean much.

Whoever caused the pain
Was not aware of it.
He may explain, apologize.
It was a great mistake without a doubt.

Look up, take a deep breath.
Not all the chances lost.
He's coming back, tomorrow.
God will see to that.

The Dawn

Like a first breath over the fields
Dawn is cutting in creepily
In shy and slow motion
Rolling its cape over the snowy landscape

Freezing birds come out of their hiding
And in sudden joy fly in little flocks chirping
Announcing the break of day
Comforting the morning

The giant prairie stands poised and still
Glorious in the first rays of morning sun
Showing the aura in its full splendour
Playing its image in full screen

Farmer's Mother

I have seen your hands at work,
How strong and swift but delicate enough.
Carrying a load of hardship in your life
Threading through the fingers and palms

I am full of sorrow looking at your hands
Wrinkled and bruised.
Unthinkable amount of work
The amount of love they shared

Early mornings filled with chores.
Longs days of genuine work
In field or in the garden
Tending and moving in a slow but steady rhythm

Night comes and your hands are not resting
They are over a sick child with fever
Caressing his forehead
Tenderly

Your magic hands are so precious
They are worn and paper thin skin
You showed all your love and sacrifice
And we can only kiss your hand

Reminiscence of the Grain Fields

An ocean of vibrant colours
Open to a view of God's splendour
Stretches to the far horizon,
Luring your eyes with all the riches

The mosaic of green and gold
Entwined with blue and yellow
The sky is bowing to take a closer look
At this human careful work

The beauty of the golden wheat
Swaying and dancing in the gentle breeze
Changing shades with every bit of blow
Whispering a voice of promise

The lively colour of yellow
Suddenly striking in the midst of green
Trying to brighten the monotony of the prairies
Even the blues calmly and shyly standing up

I am walking alongside the golden wheat field
Barren with swollen, heavy kernels
Like the joy of nature
Like the taste of bread

Meadowlark's Song

Laying in the grass and listening
Communicating with the universe
My life is full of good feelings
The moment I see a meadowlark

I do not feel alone
The cosmic exchange of words
The meadowlark's singing, relentlessly up above
Guiding me, watching over me

I take this greatest gift in
Locked deeply in my soul
Never wanting to forget it
Forever drawing it in my memory

Where were you last summer
Where were you last summer
And the great cosmos talking
And the universe watching

My Path

Foggy morning, on a wet road
An overnight shower, a scent of rain in the air
Droplets hanging on tree branches
Like tears the wind left alone

The road is steep and far
The fog too dense to see through
Yet you must take
The one that is not easy

Patches of fog lifting up, letting the sunshine in.
Far away geese flying in flocks.
Hills are getting steeper,
And the road is long and tiresome

And many hills ahead of you
And more and more you got to climb
Some steeper then the others
Some clouds of fog, yet behind

The road gets easier now
And you can see it straight ahead
The sun rays peek through
And you are guided by the angels

Child's Eyes

Just looking in the window
Seeing far away, thinking.
Is it my day, I can claim
For things are going to unveil

I see my father holding me on his lap
Teaching to write the first letters
His wisdom sinking deeply in my mind
His enormous love for his child

My childhood years are full of adventures
My happiness of today, the reflection of the past
Things we were doing are my inspiration
And the places we were seeing forever intact

We had God's abundance
The children's play and friendship
The love of neighbours and their kindness
The joy of orchards and fields

Granny's gentle, sweet care
Mother's simple scolding and singing
The way she laughed and touched
Her gentle voice was always there

Encounter

Amongst the crowd, I am rushing
My busy thoughts were on nothing
A woman stops by me just talking
And I realize she is the person.

I am still engaged, my friends are still smiling
When I get up I am drawn towards a corner
Where I see the friendly woman
I had just met before.

We know each other a few seconds
And suddenly there is a connection
It is a divine power we were given
My clear mind leads me to my angel

The words we have spoken
And her beautiful face that was telling me
Some divine message I could not understand
The so short moment lasted an eternity

I realize that I was given grace
The simple woman who spoke to me the unspoken
To feel blessed, to feel her care
She is my angel, I have been looking for her
everywhere

Day of Angels

Hectic hours have rolled by,
And I take a break to pray
To thank the Almighty for all the things
For all that I am, for all that I have

I am in the centre of all the lights around me
And the brightness of the altar
The calmness and security of church
The closeness of my love beside

God's words are spoken here
With love and understanding
The little girl's face in smiles
Like cherub holding her special charm

We both listen to the words of wisdom
God's message that fills our hearts
The little cherub claps her hands
Her angelic face with an encouraging grace

Little Angel

It is your face, of a little child
That draws all my attention
The curls around the face, with chubby cheeks
And eyes full of great joy and contentment

Your father is holding you in his arms
Clinging to you with all his love
And you return this love your own way
By emanating it to all congregation

Though precious your smile and face
Your little spirit most influential
Your sparkling eyes show us faith and hope
An amazing gift we can't go without

My friend by my side praying
We both are fascinated with the little angel
Dressed in a white gown and God's aura
So pure and innocent, will always be remembered

The power of life, the power of love
The sense of being together
I am grateful for showing me it all
Through the eyes of a little angel

In Touch

On a Lazy day across the town I wonder
Searching in my soul for the source
Tearing it apart, looking for the cause
Of pain, turmoil, grief and my own being

How can I cope these days?
My thoughts are reeling
As if the horrible wind rushed in
With a roar and powerful thunder

Have I done all good deeds?
Was I helpful and inspired many?
Have I passed enough love around?
Did I share a piece of my soul with others

These will be the questions unanswered
As only my consciousness may whisper
The sound of truth or doubt
I might have done un-imaginary

I have tried to be humble always
Taking God's guidance into consideration
And if I failed in moments of vanity
May He forgive me, and my simple errors

Negotiating this with my spirits
I feel I open my soul to the heavens
And let them judge me
If there is goodness of Thee

Ad Memoriam

And slain they were...
The children with dark eyes
And dead they were...
In rows and rows of tragic days

Surrounded by barbed wire
Closed in without a chance.
Condemned and isolated
Their bodies shriveled, bare

Their mothers denied mother's care
And children took away from mothers
There were no more tears to be shed
The sun stopped shining in those days

It is a time for a prayer
For those who were sent to death
Those whose dignity was taken away
Those who were rejected and to their sentence left

Auschwitz, Buchenwald, Majdanek, Belzec, Sobibor
The horrors of human wrong-doing
The times of hatred and human madness
Millions mercilessly perished

The rows of human shoes, human hair
The rows of human glasses. And despair...
And babies' dolls with children gone
A shriek inside your soul, the image for a lifetime

Tears are streaming down without end
Children's eyes are closed
The echo of the horror days constant
Carved in memory, only to be exposed

God of all the people
Give us the strength to go on
Forgive us our trespasses
Let us be human again, Requiem to all

Tangled Thoughts

I live in the modern world
Where things are put first
Every day is a question never answered
What is important?

The mornings are happy
The sun is always bright, hopeful
Every day in my lifetime tells me
I am God's creation

I deserve your attention
As I have a deepest connection
My feelings are always with you
Are you watching from above?

This day has unraveled slowly
There was something to do!
And there were tears of disappointment
Is it your way of telling me to honour?

Bad memories came to surface
Things happened a long time ago
Cruel, heartless and demonic
The shadows of evil people

Almighty has power to take it all back
To wipe my tears away
To bring back my faith in people
Making me important to the universe

A Land Of Promise

We've come to the open arms of the blue skies
The enormous piece of land given to us
Far beyond horizon in God's understanding
The welcome home to so many nations

We've come from Greece, Germany and Sweden
And poor lands of so many countries
France, Ukraine and Russia, Italy and Poland
From every corner of the globe

With hope, expectations and anticipation
So many of us with so little
Bare hands that took the axe
Rough, callus covered, but with a dream

We've fallen in love with the land
Giving and nurturing every moment
We took gentle care of hill
Every field and shaped it with our breath

We've thrived with our work.
Day after day, sweat dust and endurance
And only nature rewarding, compelling.
Was it His inspiration?

Dear Almighty, when you created this land
Have you measured that much for human hands?
If so, it was just right
We cannot thank you enough

Black Madonna

Salve Regina from the Mountain of Czestochowa
Your eyes and arms embrace us
You are our source of strength
And anchor of our forefathers

Throughout the centuries you showed us
Your concern and protection
And we as little children
Kneel to your feet in our need

History gales and age-long violent attacks
Did not lessen your grandeur
Or diminish neither your dignity nor your everlasting glory
We adore you

Your face scarred by enemy's sword
And despite our agony and fright
You gave us courage and verity
In struggle for our homeland

When the Swedish fierce you had seen
Burnt and plundered our land
And Turkish swords aimed at us all around
You stood on guard for our freedom

You gave our leaders great wisdom
That turned the enemies to ashes
And us a gift of power
Defending our boundaries in Thy command

Resurrected
Over a century of the partitions and our nation annihilation
Polish language dying
But never the spirit that was to be again transfigurated

Your scarred face became our shield
In defense against the attackers
When in the sea of death we were almost exterminated
You came to our Salvation

Like Phoenix from the dungeons of darkness
Our Eagle has risen. You sculptured Pilsudski's figure
His sword cut out our freedom
And he, laid on the gun-carriage, entered the eternity

Spring on the Prairie

The rolling hills turning into flat
Where deer roam free
The slough where ducks swim among the cat tails
The buzzing of a bumblebee.

The geese walk gracefully in pairs
Trying to find the best spot for the nests
Robins hop happily on their long legs
Chirping of thrushes, jays, warblers, wrens.

Goldfinches hide their nests carefully
Blackbirds watch each other
From the top of the marsh,
All that in perfect background of green grass.

Even frogs started their own melody
Not wanting to be singled out
In joyful ceremony of spring
Playing the concert to all living things

The warmth, long anticipated
Touches every flower every brush and tree
Like with a magic wand
It brings world's beauty and lays it by your feet

Czarna Madonna

Wielka Pocieszycielko, uswiecona korona,
Stoisz na Czestochowskiej Gorze przez wieki jak opoka.
Twe oczy I ramiona dla nas wsparciem,
Dodaja pokoleniom niezbadanej mocy.

Przez wieki nam mowilas
Jaka troska I ochrona Twoja trwala
A mysmy, jak male dzieci
Lgneli do Twych stop w kazdej potrzebie.

Wichry historii I potezne wrogie nawaly
Nie pomniejszyly wielkosci Twojej,
Ani nie uszczknely dostojnosci,
Nigdy nie odebraly Ci naleznej chwaly.

Miecz wroga zostawil na Twej twarzy blizne,
A Ty, pomimo cierpien I trwogi
Jak natchnienie okazalas nam wizje
Wiernosci I odwagi w kazdych dziejach narodu zmogi!

Widzialas wielu szwedzkich wrogow
Co Polske pozoga I grabieza rujnowali.
Bylas z name gdy tureckie szable
Wolnosc przez pare wiekow probowaly nam odebrac.

Dalas nam hetmanow I krolow madrosci wielkiej
Co potege wroga w puch rozniesli
I obdarzylas w polskie armie
Broniace granic w imie Twoich piesni.

I razem z name przetrwalas
Przez ponad wiek narodu unicestwienia
Gdy zanikala polska mowa –
Ale nigdy duch, ktory czekal przeistoczenia.

Gdy z mrokow niewoli trzeba bylo powstac
Ty swoja reka wyrzezbilas Pilsudskiego postac,
Ktory wlasna szabla niepodleglosc Ojczyzny wykrzesal,
A na lawecie lezac w holdzie - w poczet krolow sie zapisal.

Twa blizna byla dla nas wyzwaniem
W zmaganiach z germanskim I sowieckim najazdem,
Gdy trzeba bylo morze ofiar poniesc,
Gdy prawie braklo ludzkiej sily - Ty zstapilas.

I obdarzylas nas synem na miare tysiacleci,
Pielgrzymem narodu na najwyzszym tronie,
Ktorego slowa `` nie lekajcie sie `` wypowiedziane z natchnieniem
Kruszyly najgrubsze mury przemocy I byly prawdy objawieniem.

Za Twoja wola jestesmy dzis narodem,
Za Twoja laska poleglym oddajemy czesc.
W historii naszej nikt nie jest rowny Tobie
Za wolna Polske dzieki nasze wez !

Za Wolnosc

Zegar wybija rowna godzine
Polonez A-dur Szopena dumnie brzmi.
Te dzwieki tak dobrze znane Polakowi
Tak drogie, sa duchem przeszlosci.

Na falach radia plynie melodia poloneza
Dociera do miast I kazdej wsi
I przywoluje wspomnienia
Ogromu cierpien I rozlewu krwi

Pola bitewne po calym kraju rozrzucone
Setkami tysiecy rowno ustawionych krzyzow naznaczone
Pod Kockiem gdzie general Kleeberg dowodzil
Na Weterplatte - w obliczu krwawej zmogi.

Oczy zamglone I ciezkich czasow wspomnienia
Walki z wrogiem, mordow tylu bezbronnych,
Masowych okrazen, zeslan I cierpien w obozach
Kiedy miliony istnien zgasly w gazowych komorach.

Okrutne akty wroga, kominy obozow koncentracyjnych,
Zacieta walka z napastnikiem, cichy opor.
Smiertelny boj w obliczu narodu wycienczania
I tylko Pani Jasnogorska dawala sile do wytrwania.

Szeregi mlodych umieraly w Warszawskim Powstaniu
na szancach
W 44-tym wlasna piersia stawili opor w nierownej
walce
``Dzis do ciebie przyjsc nie moge``
Byla dla nich wezwaniem I ostatnia osloda.

Partyzanci w AK I Chlopskich Batalionach
Za ojczyzne I wolnosc swoje zycie oddali
Ich bohaterstwo , odwaga I najwyzsze poswiecenie
Na kartach historii wypisane w Virtuti Militari.

Domy I wsie spalone, miasta w ruinach
Polska dawnej swietnosci wyniszczona
Wojskowe rogatywki z orlem na polach bitew samotne
zostaly
I tylko smutne wierzby nad nimi plakaly.

Dzwieki Szopena brzmia glosno I dostojnie,
Sla ukojenie I przeslanie do naszych pokolen serc
Zwyciezylismy. Jestesmy wolni.
Nasz nakaz - wolnosci strzec.

Cornered Within

I have started an explosion
That was asleep in the depth before
They came out in sudden burst of joy
Driving all my forces to the top.

Nothing is simple anymore nor straight
One thing complicates with the other even worse I am
caught in the chain of events
I never thought I had power to forego.

When I looked in his eyes
I could see he was my extreme
Not much life was left in them
Not a spark, not glow, nor zest.

I felt sorry for his lonely life
And I had to turn it right around
God was whispering "do it"
Just to give him hope and lift him off the ground.

So I followed His sacred direction
Never thinking He might have had His way
Of showing me the perfect man
With whom my life seems not long enough.

These days I may burn in flames
My head is spinning I am dizzy
The feelings overpower me
I am cornered within

No stopping now, deeper and further
My chariot is moving in the sky
The two stars on first day we had met
Were shining at us and gave us a sign.

The Inspiration

Oh, great spirit of the nation,
We listen to you from everywhere.
Scattered around the globe,
Our thread of life we cling to, strong.

Poland's history marked with blood,
You led us through all hardship,
The darkest dungeons of our life
We had to endure to come out alive.

The years of imposed rule
When thoughts of freedom and language were dying off,
Uprising Of 1831 and rebellion of 1848
Crushed with a brutal force.

Kosciuszko's resurrection of 1794
That called the whole nation
To rise against the oppressors
With scythes and bare hands to defend.

Over the centuries Polish kingdom thrived.
The land of work, prayer and people kind
Where the love of neighbour came first
And a morning prayer was a must.

Revolutionary etude comes with a fury and blast,
An imperative to defend, to fight.
The notes are jumping madly, fast-
The recollection of the battles of the past.

The nation divided among three powers-
From being oppressed, persecuted,
Close to annihilation - has risen.
The spirit has survived on your motives and prayers.

Great patriot, who loved every meadow, stream,
Every hill, willows, the folklore of the village,
Forever resonating the beauty of this country's spirit
Embedded deeply in his timeless, Polish genius.

An absolute during wars' bloodshed
When millions fought and perished,
To those who survived
His music was daily bread.

The Funeral March to all Poles we play,
Those deported to Siberia thousands of miles,
Those, who in the battle of Monte Cassino, Narvik,
London,
Tobruk, Kock, Kolobrzeg, Warszawa for freedom died.

We pay our utmost tribute to you.
Your genius has been our rock.
Your music extraterrestrial and eternal
Goes on, and on, and on....

The Notion

From scratch I got to gather myself,
To pick my own pieces,
To put them together
And breathe, function, have faith.

My father's teaching, his wisdom
So deeply embedded in me,
My whole foundation for life,
I now chip off that strength piece by piece at a time.

Act on love, build out of love.
No greater power, without an end,
A circle, a perfect dimension-
Invisible, yet expressed in so many ways.

I am whimpering, chirruping as a little bird,
My uneasiness comes as a cloud.
Distracted in the past, tears flowing,
The burden too heavy over the love lost.

I claim my power holding it strong,
The wonders I created on it alone.
Eternal, endearing and tender,
Love that binds us and has no regrets.

The Sower

The farmer's hands touched the earth,
Transfigurating it with love.
The seeds have been dropped in the ground
Giving the beginning to the cycle of life.

The dream is unveiling,
The sun adds magic brightness to it,
Warmth looks after all tenderly
With an array of shades of green.

A symphony of life burst out,
Giving a shape to stems and twigs,
Forming the buds with magnificent, careful art,
Covering the black earth in an accompaniment.

The hands that sowed have been resting,
All pains taken turned into great deeds.
The summer solstice has blessed the crops
In wonder of the sower's work for humanity.

The Wheat Fields

It is time to seed again,
The ground is soft and fertile, awaiting.
The black earth rested all winter long
Just to be sawn and from anew born.

The wanderers of the world came here
To this beauty constantly drawn.
The majestic land of open skies,
Rivers, hills and steppes adorned.

The black fields unmeasured in size,
Producing, giving in abundance,
Providing to the hungry, always,
The wheat we've worshipped for life.

We treasure this God's gift to all people,
Humbly bending to work this land
With hours of labour and heavy sweat,
The sun and wind its caress.

The enormous fields, summer blessed
And someone was tending them
To our contentment and plenty,
Made wheat kernels long and straight.

In even rows it grows in amazement,
Getting higher, changing its colour to gold,
A promise of wonders to all human beings.
The sky stretched its starry cape over it, in awe.

Through The Rain

In the rain drops a sunray glitters,
Very small but visible,
Like my anticipation of better future
That is yet supposed to be.

Shivering and trembling
I wrap myself up in a blanket,
Full of good memories and bad,
Trying to sort them out and forget.

The hardship has faded away,
The troubles insignificant, defeated.
People from the past rejected and erased.
I am longing for the unknown to become.

My heartache seems to subside,
Staying only deep and pulsing.
I am so fragile, so weak,
Afraid to open it up and tear it out.

The rain drops have stopped falling,
The last few ones joined together in a tiny riel.
When tomorrow comes and clear the mind
This troubled day will be washed out.

Through the Tunnel

I jumped on the train and took off,
My journey full of bumps and turns,
Across the ocean, mountains and plains'
Faster and faster, away I went.

The scenery is moving in front of my eyes,
Children playing with flying kites.
The quiet country road dividing the fields,
The enormous sky. And the train picks up speed.

It takes me to the places of beauty,
Over the rivers and busy towns,
The inseparable baggage of life becomes lighter,
Moving towards my last stop.

The tunnel comes suddenly like trauma,
With darkness, holding me in a grip,
A choking sensation of drowning, fright, blindness,
Pain, the excruciating pain and sadness.

I am passive, shaken, can hardly breathe.
The wheels go fast in a noisy rhythm.
The moment the radiant sun appears my fears are
over,
My happiness comes from within.

Travel

Wandering between two worlds,
Crossing the ocean of human emotions,
I know how fragile is my being.
Yet I try to explore the sense of it all.

I talk to strangers, curious,
What their life is like,
When they make me laugh or smile
I feel I travel, among their souls I abide.

I long for my childhood years,
Nostalgia is in my heart a frequent guest,
For I have not forgotten the kindness of people
Nor the scent of earth in those days.

And, so I travel, in time and my mind,
Reaching out to the people.
Looking for the threading that connects
The past and the present, while the worlds slowly roll by.

Wierzby Szopena

Tworco nut piekna, wirtuozie poezji ducha,
Od najwczesniejszych lat dzieciecych Twoja muzyka
Zapadla gleboko w moje serce
I na zawsze tam juz pozostanie, na glucho...
Niebianska sztuka twoja wiedzie mnie przez zycie,

Jest zarem palacym i wszystkim co wyobraznia zamarzy.
Kazda nuta do mnie przemawia, uskrzydla,
I rysuje dzwiekami fortepianu polskie obrazy.

Mazurek plynie jak lany zboza z wiatrem falujace,
Przeskakuje po pagorkach, potokach i dolinach i
widoki maluje swojskie.
Z oddali glosy kukulki i slowikow slychac rzewne trele,
i ostrzonej kosy,
Wiesniakow schylonych na polu i ich odglosy.

Walc wiruje i porywa do tanca,
Kolem sie toczy jak westchnienie,
I uderza do glowy - pociaga, pochlania, zniewala,
odurza,
Az brakuje oddechu i popadasz w zatracenie.

Preludium zawodzi teskna melodia w przestworzach,
Po sciezkach i polnych miedzach sie wije,
Jak lza po twarzy splywa. Nuty porwal wicher
I rzucil w dalekie przestrzenie za morza.

Klawiszow grzmot potezny sie rozpetal, burza z furia
uderza,
Polonez A-dur wybija narodu dume i odwage.
W marmurze nasz znak wolnosci, bialy orzel,
Co zawisl wysoko nad polskim krajobrazem.

Utulasz mnie w berceusy nutach slodkich,
Gdy zmysly moje utajone w ciszy drgaja, jecza,
A zal, tesknota i rozterka do konca nie siegaja.
I urzeczony tylko jestem; wiezniem.

Wykules naszego ducha w wielu zbrojnych porywach,
A kiedy nadeszla godzina trwogi Polski udreczonej
Dales nam wiare w nasze sily i ukazales do
niepodleglosci droge,
Jak haslo do walki do ostatniego tchu niezlomnej.

Tys naszego ducha narodu uosobieniem.
W delikatnych dotknieciach sonaty wierzby pochylone,
W deszczu kroplach cichy placz i ukojenie,
I nawet bociany brodzace po lace w nia zasluchane.

Gwiazdy zamarly i wisza na niebie nieruchomo,
W ich blasku powiew etiudy promieniuje,
Coraz dalej i wyzej siega, rozsyla ja w pozaswiaty,
Wsrod nich Twoja gwiazda najwieksza, cudowny czariot
w konstellacji.

Wyjales moje zycie i w swojej dloni piescisz,
A ja jak male kukle kwile i wszystko zapominam.
Z otchlani, z chaosu moje mysli wydobywasz,
Zamet, bol, niepokoj roztapia sie, rozplywa.

A jesli smutek mnie otoczy czy nostalgia trzyma,
Nokturnem rozdzierasz w strzepy drobne moje serce,
I juz nie widze konca, i slucham cie... i Trwam na
zawsze...i spelniam sie..
Pianissimo...pianissimo...pianissimo...

Chopin's willows

Oh poet of notes of beauty, virtuoso of soul,
From my mother's womb your music
Sank deeply in my heart
And will stay there forever, intact.

Your music has led me throughout my life with a radiating force
Like an ardor and was everything you can dream of.
The nourishing tones have carried me on
Painting an unforgettable Polish scene.

The Mazurka tones flow lightly like wavy wheat fields in the wind,
Jumping over the hills, across the valleys and the streams
Painting the well known,
So dear, Polish country scenes.

Like nightingale chirruping and cuckoo's song
From far away
Blended with the sound of sharpened scythe
And quietly talking peasants bent over the field.

Waltz takes you twirling, inviting to dance,
Round and round, lightly like a sigh,
Gets to your head – attracting,
alluring, stunning, constraining

Until you are breathless, until in it you lose yourself.

Prelude sings plaintively in expanse
Through the path and ridges between the fields like a ribbon winding,
Rolls down the face like a tear. Gone with the wind
Went the notes, far across the sea and ocean.

With the keys fury and thunder
Polonaise A-dur strikes the nation's pride and courage.
The white eagle, our emblem of freedom rising
Crowned in the highest, up above the homeland.

A sweet, appeasing berceuse's sound.
My deeply hidden senses shiver, tremble and groan,
When sorrow, longing and discord never reach beyond
And I am like imprisoned, spellbound.

You sculpted our spirit in many battles and wars,
And when the bells tolled in the hour of doom -
You gave us faith and led us to our freedom,
Like a trumpet calling to invincible fight till the last breath.

You are the nation spirit's impersonation.
In delicate sonata touches willows bending low,
Quiet cry, an appeasement in rain drops,
Even the wading storks in the meadow are all listening in awe.

The stars froze hanging still in the sky,
The dazzling etude is radiating in their shine,

It reaches farther and higher, sending it across the universe.
Among them your star is the greatest, a shiny chariot in the constellation.

You took my life and in your hand you're holding it,
And me, like a birdie, chirruping and forgetting it all,
Out of depths of chaos you're dragging out my thoughts,
Confusion, pain, uneasiness is disappearing,getting dissolved.

And when I'm deeply in sadness, nostalgia and oblivion
With the nocturne like with a sword you cut my heart in pieces,
And I can't see the end... and I am listening... and I am being forever...
And I exist.
Pianissimo...
Pianissimo...
Pianissimo...

Ziemia Lubelska

Poranna rosa blyszczy kroplami w trawie,
Mieni sie w rannych promieniach slonca,
Razem z ziemia oddycha. W gorze leca zurawie ,
Kwietniowe jablonie w pelni kwiecia.

Zapach ziemi po mokrym deszczu jak obietnica,
Zaorane pola stoja rzedami czarne,
Czekaja na ludzka prace, na zasiew ziarna.
Wrony po nich chodza, sprawdzaja czy to pod pszenice.

Ta ziemia taka zyzna, z troska dopatrzona,
Choc w pocie czola uprawiana
Wydaje z zadziwieneim obfite plony
Jako nagrode za trud pieczolowicie wlozony.

Pszenica na polach wzeszla niezwykle piekna,
Przez wieki z najwyzsza czcia otaczana,
A zyto, jeczmien i rzepak spiesza za nia.
Warzywa po ogrodach roznymi kolorami zadziwiaja.

Sady, o sady, cudowna won kwitnacych wisni
wydzielaja,
Kwiaty ich biale z najbielszych z rozowym wymieszane,
Jak panna mloda w slubnej sukni ubrane,
Ten widok w pamieci na dlugo zostanie.

Czeresnie, sliwy, grusze, wisnie i jablonie otulaja domy,
A kwiat ich naladowany nektarami.
Pszczoly do nich pracowicie sie zabieraja
I kazdy kwiat z niezmiernym trudem zapylaja.

Kaczence zolcia sie mienia w pelnym sloncu,
Fiolki, przylaszczki, przebisniegi, zawilce
Cicho po lasach sobie szepca,
Lilie wodne i tatarak skrywaja zaby po wodnych szuwarach.

Pomiedzy pagorkami kosciol ustawiony
I stamtad dochodzi glos porannych dzwonow.
Lud pracowity z uplecionymi wiankami na msze spieszy,
Na ustach wymawia “ Niech bedzie pochwalony “.

Bociany na dachu stodoly gniazdo uwily starannie,
W lesie dziecioly stukaja, chore drzewa sprawdzaja.
Kukulka jedna z druga kuka, kompanii szuka.
Poranny koncert wrzaskliwy roznymi tonami rozbrzmiewa, w duszy spiewa.

Strumyki Roztocza po lasach cicho szemrza,
Nad nimi odurzajacy zapach lesnych ziol i czeremchy.
Grzybow co niemiara, i paproci,
Kamienie na wpol ukryte w wodzie zapraszaja do odwiedzin.

Miasta polskie z historii tu wyrosly -
Lublin, Zamosc, Tomaszow, Chelm, Hrubieszow.

Ziemia poetow, pisarzy, naukowcow, lekarzy, inzynierow
Co rozslawili Polski nauke i sztuke za rubieza.

Zamek na wysokiej gorze w Lublinie stoi,
Wielki dowod Polski potegi i chwaly,
Goruje nad wszystkim i wydaje wyraz
Naszej swietnosci i ukochania tej ziemi i jej historii.

Helene
Montessigny-Clement
h. Zaremba – Cielecka

She emigrated from Poland to Canada in the early eighties.
She was educated in Poland with a University degree.
She raised her family in rural Saskatchewan. She lives near Saskatoon. The vastness and overwhelming beauty
of the Great Canadian Prairies has provided a lasting impression and inspiration for her writing.